Exposed: The Collected Works of
Ireana Fields

Copyright © 2016 by Ireana Fields

All rights reserved. No part of this book may be reproduced in any form or by any means without the prior written consent of the Publisher, except in the case of brief quotations embodied in critical articles or reviews.

ISBN-13: 978-0-9839187-7-6

First Printing: March 2016

Printed in the United States of America

This book is dedicated to my beautiful and charismatic daughters, Carrington and Cadence, I love you both to the moon and back. And to Sedale, I love you more than words can say...

Message to Readers

It took me a while to be able to share my private thoughts publicly. I was always afraid of how people would perceive my art; or me for that matter. Each poem I've written came from my heart. Every feeling I've felt inspired me to write, and I'm no longer afraid to show my vulnerability. This book formally introduces me to the world. In this book, I'm totally exposed.

Acknowledgements

It seems that in the past few years, my journey has been endless. I've been through a lot, which is mostly why I turned to writing and a few select people. They deserve all the thanks in the world for remaining consistent.

Carrington, you bring me life and meaning. You have so much personality and life; it's insane—never lose that. Mommy loves you so much, stink!

Cadence—your smile alone brings so much light to my life. Getting you here was a journey, but we both made it. Mommy loves you, Cay-Cay!

Sedale—our life together has been super crazy in such a short period of time. From our first conversation of going to the Isley Brothers concert, being engaged, living together, to having a baby. I'm glad to say that our love has only increased. Thanks for everything you do. I don't know what I would do without you. I love you!

Mom—you are my backbone. Life would be unbearable without you having my back. I love you to pieces (even when I get aggravated). It is because of you that I've made it this far. You are my best friend.

Nia—you were Auntie's baby before I had a baby. I love you so much, sweetie. You are so talented, intelligent, and beautiful. Never lose sight of who you are.

Sister and Alex—you guys are awesome. I love y'all. Thank you, sister, for having my back and believing in me and my dreams; I really appreciate you.

My second mom and Jay—I appreciate y'all so much. Thanks for all the advice and words of encouragement. I love y'all!

I love you, Dad.

Auntie Val and Auntie Deborah—you guys are some of my biggest supporters. Thank you for reading everything I write. I love y'all.

Mother, Auntie Wanda, and Uncle Rod—I love y'all so much.

Uncle Jr. and Uncle Narward—I have the best memories of you. I love you and I miss you.

Tassia, Ashanti, Tristian, Addie, Everett, Akeem, Mama Sophie, Uncle Bobby, Taylor, Shivon, and Phil—although I don't talk to y'all daily, I love y'all dearly. I consider y'all to be family.

Ms. Mickey—thanks for always being there for me and providing good advice and a listening ear. I love you.

Jackie—I love you to pieces. Even though we work together, I consider you to be a friend. You listen to me rant and rave, and you've been there for me through good and bad. You've provided a shoulder to cry on, a comforting back pat, and a million laughs. I love you, girl! Oh and s/o to your fam. Desmond, Jada, Jasmin, and Poonie!

Marky Poo—you are by far my best friend, my unbiological baby daddy, and my level head. You mean the world to me; I swear I couldn't make it a week without you. It's the little things like our movie days, endless conversations about conspiracy theories and the state of our people, or us simply being silly that mean the most. You are super talented and one day the entire world will know it. Thanks for giving me the most awesome book cover ever and always pushing me to pursue my dreams. You will be in my life forever and ever, so the adjustment bureau and the producers better make sure their shit is straight. xoxo.

    Any family or friends that I forgot, charge it to my mind not my heart.

    To all the men who have hurt me in any way, thank you. You've taught me awesome lessons and inspired my poetry.

    Last, and certainly not least, thank you Father God, for surrounding me with people who are genuine, taking away those who aren't, taking me through the trials, and allowing me to have triumphs as well. Without you, there is no me. I thank you, I love you, and if you never blessed me again, I'm beyond thankful for what I've already been given.

    This book represents me. To anyone that reads it, I truly thank you.

xoxo—Ireana

1- He Made Love to My Mind

Last night, I experienced something special.

I felt true love.

For the first time he made love to my mind.

Penetration wasn't needed, because his words were orgasmic.

Tears filled my eyes as his words made a connection with my heart. For a moment I felt emotionally raped, because he took my feelings and exposed them even when I said no.

However, I became vulnerable and gave into his words...I showed him me.

Every secret and hidden thought came from my lips into his mind.

We exchanged souls.

Our spirits for the first time became one.

We saw each other naked, no lies all truths, and accepted each other.

He took my hypothetical virginity, because I can now give him all of me with no hesitation.

It was hard to breathe, because every moment we shared that night took my breath away.

I think I'm becoming a nymphomaniac, because I'm addicted to his love.

Now I constantly feel him inside of me.

He's the very reason my heart beats.

I felt something so powerful, so special, so intense, and so erotic. For the first time, I felt true love, because last night he made love to my mind.

2- My Exquisite Pain

Ironically, I lied to you because you lied to me.

I closed my eyes to the sight of you just so my heart wouldn't have to face you.

I wanted you to feel my pain,

But no, you don't feel it—you couldn't possibly deal with it.

Your tears end with a smile, while my tears end with self-doubt.

Why me? Why not me? Why should I? Why couldn't I be more to you?

I jump head first into a hole of chaos I'm called a fool.

My pain and rage is rushing through my veins—to the side of my mind that's no longer logical but insane.

I love the pain…suffering is my muse.

I tie myself up so you can punish me like only a lover can do.

I'm a masochist—I yearn for your exquisite pain.

I'm ashamed to admit it, but why else would I run back to it.

I'm blinded by love. I can only see you, or at least the image I've created in my mind and pretended it was you.

If where you are is where you want to be…

Seeing how you're not here, do you really want me?

I couldn't tell

But you tease me with false hope telling me it'll be this way but it won't.

But I allow you to string me along.

My mind's made up, but my heart is undecided.

During the day I hide behind a fake smile, but at night I'm awake crying.

Why do I deal with this?

Because I want you, the better part of you;

The side that doesn't lie and treats me how you used to— when I mattered to you.

The only time you show emotion is after I cry.

Sadly, I've cried my last tear a thousand times.

I no longer believe myself.

I lie to my heart so my mind won't accept I'm drowning in stupidity.

But I don't think it's working, because my mind still has faith in love although my heart is hurting.

Why can't I leave you?

I sit by the phone waiting for your call as if I have something to say. Then I find myself swimming in disappointment when the phone hasn't rung and it's the end of the day.

Exposed

I believe I'm slightly crazy to even expose myself to such treatment.

I don't want to feel this way for the rest of my life, I want a commitment.

So why am I still here?

I've gone completely insane. I'm addicted.

I'm still tying myself up to experience your exquisite pain...

3- Dear Diary

Dear Diary, today I lost my soul mate.

Time erased every present the present time would give and all I wished I had said but was too late.

All past arguments became meaningless; all beautiful moments became distant memories.

Today my past love and ideal present became twisted, so now it's hard for me to accept our future.

Dear Diary, we are no longer an "our," him and I are no longer an "us," it's just me.

He will never know my heart; he will never know my mind; he will never truly see the real me.

I wish I could take everything back, but like me, he never forgets.

Now I have all the time in the world to sit and contemplate things I should have did or didn't do and signs I should've ignored and ones I shouldn't have missed.

Dear Diary, today I have a broken heart.

I stayed up all night crying, because it was when I rolled over to be in your arms I realized that we were apart.

Our relationship wasn't always good, but now for some strange reason I can't remember the bad.

I wish I could be with you to prove we were meant to be, but what I once said I have is now what I had.

Exposed

I know I will never love anyone the way that I love you.

Dear Diary, today I met a boy, but I will never be able to love him right because he's not you...

4- Fatal Attraction

I'm sitting here and my mind keeps drifting.

Wondering if your mind's wandering onto thoughts of me, or if you're feeling the same and it's me you're missing.

I can't understand how I allowed my mind to accept that you don't fully belong to me.

And that although you spent one beautiful night with me reality is still real and you have to leave to go to your family.

I'm sitting here, looking at your pictures,

Trying to analyze every smile, every gesture, but all I'm seeing is that you're happy in every dimension.

If only things were different, if only we met sooner,

If only a few stolen moments were constant actions rather than things I can only remember.

Still I love you, and although I can't have all of you I want a part of you.

The part of you that thinks of me, loves me, wants me, needs me, and fantasizes about me too.

I'm sitting here thinking, about the time when you belonged to me.

When you slept next to and inside of me

It was one of the best nights of my life.

Exposed

And everybody could say it's wrong, but in my mind it's right

So, I don't care. I know I occupy your mind even when we're apart.

I know where I belong...In the corner crack of the closet in your heart.

5- For the One Who Reads What I Write

For the one who reads what I write, you've touched me in many ways.

You forced me to really see myself and develop a "cocky" mentality, so I won't feel ashamed.

When I wake you're the first thought that crosses my brain, and I wait for your messages.

I had a city built around my heart, a million walls up, yet and still you made it in.

For the one who reads what I write, I want to have you wide open as if I mentally fucked you.

Invade your thoughts, and cause a constant flow of emotions as if I'm performing tantric sex on you.

I want to say and do all the right things to you. Stroke your ego…slowly. Hypothetically make love to you.

For the one who reads what I write, I want the type of love that's considered "old school"

Where I check yes in the box, after the question do I like you?

I want to provide fantasies that will become indelibly placed on your mind

Where they are played sporadically in your head and when it's over you press rewind.

Exposed

For the one who reads what I write, you are the perfect lyric over any beat.

"Could this be love?" because nothing else "tastes this warm, or feels this sweet"

"in my mind, I'll always be his lady" and I'll never "let go."

I love you...and there's something you should know...

For the one who reads what I write, you're the reason I write.

6- Replaced

Replaced...Without a trace of emotion

"no name" saved in your brain, just let go...

But where did it go?

Was I simply misplaced or just erased?

Or is your mind now on other things, other than me...Or could it be that—

The panties were too lace, and now your mind's laced with thoughts of them...

Although I could do it better,

Whether or not you believe it, I could show you better.

Sittin' by the phone is getting a bit redundant,

Especially since it hasn't rung yet.

Racking my brain trying to comprehend or at least slightly understand it

Why haven't I heard from you in 2 days, 48 hours, 2880 minutes to be specific?

Out of frustration I'm screaming...Are you even listening?

Is there still an image of me on your brain, or are you seeing through me as if I'm cellophane?

Looking right through me with your eyes closed...literally.

Hypothetical excuses used to fill my head with the "what

ifs" to somewhat accept reality

Setting myself up to believe the detailed stories that begin with "what had happened was" although the person telling them is usually lying.

So I guess I just have to accept that I was replaced... Without a trace of emotion

"no name" saved in your brain, and just simply let go...

7- Pro Choice?

The easiest thing to do is the hardest to conceive.

But physically conceiving was better.

Tears streaming down my face uncontrollably, my pillow's wetter and wetter.

"They" say there are options, but are they really worth taking?

Thinking loud thoughts that may not be worth saying, my mind's made up, but it's still the "options" that it's weighing.

Feeling insane because every time I close my eyes I'm hearing a vacuum suck away the life that had a right but I took away.

Watching what I say aloud so "I can't have you" won't be the last thing my child hears me say.

How can it be that my selfish reasons also display selflessness?

I still can't decide if this is something I'll live to regret… but at least I'll have the chance to live.

Never will I hear you cry, your first words, see your face, or lay you in your crib.

But I'm supposed to be your mother…mothers are nurturing.

Watching the news in disgust but it's my own child I'm murdering.

Dreading morning sickness but it may be better than sickness from mourning.

Life is valuable; the cost of abortion is high. But honestly speaking even if it was free could I mentally afford it?

Recurring nightmares of holding my child's hand at a tombstone, telling him it will be okay while he wept.

Laid him in a casket and closed it while he slept.

All because his life isn't convenient but life isn't convenient.

I took his away before he had a chance.

Because I couldn't sacrifice my life to give my child life…I gave it death.

8- I Promised I Would Finish It

He said:

Damn, you're beautiful...

And I haven't even had the opportunity to explore anything

On the exterior of your endoskeleton;

I mean your inner beauty is truly evident and present in

Your very essence but good heavens I've never witnessed such elegance by the section without sex involved.

For you have a gift that I would never even attempt to taint

With my tattered temple...

His words spoke to me, blinded me, excited me, and showed me his soul.

Intimacy is one thing but to connect with someone abruptly, and to vividly depict forthcoming is insane

But who needs logic when we're so in sync.

Your heart is of one I've never witnessed, uniqueness is what you possess, able to imagine feelings expressed through your caress.

I cringe, not because I'm disgusted but because this is an area no one has touched.

And, I have been mentally stimulated...I could never be

tainted.

Imagination is what I use to see what would happen if we set no boundaries and limits referred to the restraints I used to tie you up.

But simply sleeping in your arms is enough to make me never want to wake up.

Perpetual bliss in the moment we kissed feelings as if nothing else matters, and it's in our own world that we exist.

Sex is highly overrated when you can feel mentally ignited.

Wishing we could experience forever and never end up divided.

You have truly sparked my curiosity and invaded my thoughts.

I fell in love with you...

9- Laughing

You are fucking hilarious...

By every standard.

No need to deny it, as long as you're satisfied with being asinine, it's fine.

Do you...like only you can.

Or at least be the person you want other people to think you are and when you piss them off you blow it off as if they just don't understand.

Hiding behind complexity when in all actuality you're as transparent as cellophane.

Acting as if I don't know your name...I know your full name, address, birth date, social security number, likes, dislikes, I know you better than you.

The true you...that is.

The one that chases pussy like it's a sport, breaking hearts, telling lies until you find someone to support you.

You think the coochie is platinum; I personally think it should get appraised.

Telling lies, playing on my intelligence as if I'm insane!

Thinking if you change your personality and Facebook name that makes you transformed, but really you're just inane

Lacking significance, depth, just plain lacking.

So while you're doing your transformations, manipulating, and lying I'm laughing.

You think I can't see you for who you are? You're as opaque as glass.

I know your past, present, and future to be exact.

Predictability in your life has never been overlooked.

I know everything you've done and will do as if I've read your life story in a book.

You should really try to be original.

10- I Was Once Told I Was Loved

I was once told that I was beautiful.

I would be stared at for hours. I was a work of art; he said he never saw a vision so incredible.

So he bought me...I became his.

He carefully placed me on his wall and said he would keep me forever. He said he knew where home is.

But as soon as I was hung my value depreciated, because it wasn't fully appreciated.

I became just another work of art in his museum of the broken hearted.

I was once told that forever was in my eyes;

That words couldn't verbalize what was being said in my expression.

And every time we made love every moan I produced sounded like heaven.

He said he could get lost in my eyes

And I suppose he did...

He vanished.

I was once told that I was cared for;

That it was I he yearned for.

Adored and adorned with the best, because he said that

Exposed

was what I deserved.

Captivated by bliss, the line between fantasy and reality, I couldn't discern.

He told me he would keep my heart safe, that he would never break it.

But it was he who broke it.

I was once told that I was loved...

11- Thinking of Him All Day

Thinking of him all day; wondering if I'm in his thoughts. I think I'm becoming obsessed....callin' all day just to hear his voice, or even his voicemail.

Dropped my walls, opened up, not afraid to tell him things I wouldn't usually tell,

But he's got me that way.

I'm feeling like a kid again, up late talking, fallin' asleep on the phone,

Feeling so right not wanting to acknowledge any sign that maybe wrong

Sporadically, daydreaming of the day I'll meet you at the altar in a princess-like white dress.

Please believe I'm so in love, so if you send me a letter asking me that question, I would check the box marked "yes."

I'm so ready.

Even though we argue sometimes, I wouldn't want it any other way.

Regardless of what some might say. Me being a woman, I love when my man puts me in my place.

By his side is where I reside from now until death do us part.

Here is where I want to be, because I only want the one who has my heart.

12- Untitled

Darkness has filled my heart and I'm left lonely.

With faces of rejection, there is no familiar face of someone to console me.

Clinching no hand for help, no one helps because they can't hear my silent screams.

Is it because I'm the woman in your dreams that you can't see because you're still asleep?

Hell, you couldn't handle my spirit and my heart is one thing you can't keep.

I'm always dealing with the brothas who claim they're different and they'll do the things other niggas won't.

Got more drama than the news; thugging, hustling, pimping, or straight mentally and spiritually broke.

Where's that Wall Street brotha with the funds to take care of me?

Or the hardcore thug with wife beaters, Timbs, and Girbaud jeans?

Where's that Romeo-type that worships me and lives to see me another day?

Or the clown-type dude that I can chill with, trip with, and play?

Why can't I find someone for me, take care of me, benefit me, intrigue me, and compel me with his personality?

Maybe it's because I see faces of rejection and there's no familiar face to console me.

Clinching no hand for help, no one helps because they can't hear my silent screams.

13- My Love for You

This metaphysical state of euphoria has got me partially insane;

Enamored by your touch, the feeling of bliss in your kiss, becoming mentally challenged just by the sound of your name,

This is more than just the word "love" it's a state of being.

It's the air in my lungs, the persistent thought in my head, the eroticism of lust, the romance and passion in love, seeing and believing.

I let go of my past and gave up on negativity.

I was truly given a gift because you're in my presence, and I envision you in my future. You're my ending and beginning.

You are a perfect reflection of everything I wanted and required things beyond my comprehension.

Memories indelibly placed on my brain and in my heart is all of my emotions felt and an accurate depiction.

Feeling basically psychotic as if I'm emotionally stalking, because I can't get you out of my brain.

In your words, I'm "emotionally fucked"

Every time we're together it's like an outer body experience...living in a dream and I don't ever want to wake up.

Existing isn't enough; I want to dwell in your reality.

Where love and happiness do exist dually and feelings are felt mutually.

Yes, I would run away with you, and jump off a cliff if you said you could fly.

And I wouldn't sit it out I would dance with you every time because I trust you with my spirit, heart, soul, and mind.

I feel like you were made for me, in every way possible.

So if it takes forever to earn your love and trust, then I don't mind because all I want is you.

14- Who Am I?

I can't comprehend how it is that you still affect my emotion

When love has been gone, along with honesty, respect, and devotion.

Do you know how many times I've stayed awake crying?

Calling you, asking when you'd be home? Knowing everything you said in response would sound like you're lying.

But still I put my feelings to the side and put on a smile when you'd walk through the door.

And when we made love, the thoughts of you being with someone else, I'd try to ignore.

For the longest time I wondered why I wasn't good enough or what was it that I did or didn't do.

So I tried to change. I tried to be more quiet, more understanding, and better looking. But I lost myself trying to be perfect for you.

Who am I now? I only remember who I was.

I spent so long trying to be the perfect wife for you, but who am I without you? What's an effect without a cause?

15- The Mistress

He kissed me, caressed me, and it meant so much.

Fantasized of what could've been, felt lust in your touch.

You go through my mind sporadically throughout the day and night.

Visions of us being together and everything between us made right.

We have the perfect relationship; we understand each other because we are good friends.

And when we make love to each other it's powerful and passionate; I wish it would never end...

But it always does no matter how much I dream and fantasize, you aren't mine.

And you could never fully be committed to me, because you have to go home to your wife.

And although it's wrong I can't suppress my feelings.

And she would never understand why I want her husband or the thoughts in my mind I constantly deal with.

This isn't about hurting her; its' about wanting him.

It's the desire I feel below my waist, the shiver down my spine, the sensation of placing my pillow case on my face just to smell him.

I'm simply infatuated and I don't care who knows.

But to him I'm his secret that he'd prefer no one to know.

So he hides me, we just meet whenever he has spare time.

Because never will he fully be with me or love me,
because for better or for worse he'll be with his wife.

16- Untitled

Tears on my pillow, crying from my soul

Nobody understands my feelings, no one knows.

Screaming and shouting, but no one can hear.

I feel like I'm separated; like I'm far and they're near.

Nobody understands my dreams and my ambitions.

They talk so much, like they know what's up, but they don't care to listen.

17- Caged

Caged and unable to see the world

Unable to express myself

Unable to find happiness.

Lonely and alone.

Lifeless and dull.

Separated and discreet.

Always wondering, never finding answers.

Searching in darkness, never finding light.

Eyes wide shut.

Blinded by reality but wide awake in my dreams.

I'm a lonely bird ready to fly, but caged.

18- Unread

I'm living an unread book, trying to find an indefinite conclusion.

Speaking loudly but silent.

Misunderstood but judged.

Hurt but painless.

Is it worth it?

Living without cause? Guessing without probability?

Heartaches of rejection and stirred to mindlessness.

Hope follows, but reality calls.

Expect nothing...

19- Crazy or Insane

Ladies and gentlemen of the jury, I'm going to tell you my story; because how could you judge me if you don't even know me? This justifies my crime; this is what I said that night...

I'm in love with you, so I just can't say no.

And it's so funny how I follow you no matter where you go.

Sometimes I feel like taking a knife and slitting your throat.

And when I go to court I'll plead guilty, because I have no self-control.

See, being with you is a love-hate type of thing.

But I'll let you be the judge on whether I'm crazy or insane.

Sometimes I want to shoot you and bury your body under the soil.

And when someone mentions you I'll say I never knew you.

You work me up, but you bring me back down.

You're like a fucking elevator making its rounds.

See, I trusted you with my heart and you just stepped on it.

I wish I could make a dent on your face and we'll see

who'll be crying then.

I loved you and you'd rather leave me alone and make me cry.

If I had a gun, I'd shoot nine rounds in your chest and watch your stupid ass die.

I can't stand what you do; you make me feel so unreal.

But this pain you put me through no one can feel.

I could cry a million black tears and you wouldn't wipe away one.

But once I decapitate you, who the fuck will feel dumb?

You're losing grip on a handle that you truly can't hold.

You might as well let go because my heart is getting cold.

People of the jury, I did what I did.

Hypothetically speaking, his life just had to end.

Since I warned him many times, my motive won't change…

But you be the judge…

Am I crazy or insane?

20- You Crossed My Mind

You crossed my mind...actually to be quite clear, you stayed there.

I fell for you even before I was aware.

Now my constant fear is living my life without you and not having you near.

It may seem insane to feel so strong,

But right or wrong, I want my heart to reside with you, for a term that is long.

You complete me, love me, excite me, and humor me; make me feel free.

Without you I couldn't breathe,

And I wouldn't want to.

My love is yours, it can't be replaced.

And to ask how much I love you...let me count the ways.

It's immeasurable; it would take days—an infinite amount of time would pass before I could even verbalize what to say.

My love is real, and lying staring in your eyes it's apparent.

My happiness with you is evident and consistent—it could never be sporadic.

But my love is not perfect, nothing is, but it's worth it.

21- Confused

So is this you?

Because this "you" is completely different from whom I once knew.

Maybe I was mistaken… I guess it's possible. The years that have passed was a lie

Or was I simply lying to myself? I suppose I wasn't the one—or at least not the one you wanted. I can't decide.

If I would've known that I would feel this exact way at this precise time, I would've let go before we began.

I hid you in the part of my mind that memories are placed. You were almost erased, but seeing you in front of my face I began to remember all of the lies you once said.

For a moment I hurt.

I couldn't process the sight….

Now all I'm wondering is why?

22- For Him

For whatever reason, I can't tell you how I feel.

And no matter how much I try to come up with an accurate description, it seems damn near impossible, because the only thing that can truly depict it is real.

My heart feels full, because it's no longer broken.

I feel like I've finally found true love, so there's no way I could ever be lonely.

It is you that I truly love.

Being hurt a million times was worth it to experience your love at least once.

To finally understand what it means for souls and spirits to be exchanged from one simple touch.

I crave you.

There aren't enough hours in the day to be around you.

I can talk to you for hours at a time and still get butterflies when I see your name in my call log; I swear I could never get tired of you.

I've never been completely sure about someone, felt complete love, or knew complete happiness until the day you completed me.

And even though I can't predict the future, I know by your side is where I always want to be.

There will never be enough words, enough time, enough

thought, or enough courage to say all that I want to.

So the only way to say it simply is that for now and always, I will love you.

23- In A Perfect World

In a perfect world,

We would be together,

Deep in love, bliss in every touch, ties that cannot be severed.

In a perfect world,

There's just me; I'm the only one you see.

Math is very basic; there are no additional multiples, just you and me.

In a perfect world,

You are here by my side, night after night you hold me tight.

It's the closeness you provide. In your arms nothing's wrong, everything's all right.

In a perfect world,

Negative words don't slip from our lips.

We use them to kiss, not dismiss.

In a perfect world,

I am appreciated; I'm needed and never taken for granted.

Our love will remain vibrant, never fading.

But the sad truth is that this is reality.

You don't see me, and probably never will.

I gave you my love, you played with my feelings, and it's my heart that you killed.

In reality,

We don't talk.

We converse now and then until you randomly cut me off.

Then I'm stuck, trying to figure out why.

Lying down at night, telling my heart lies, sighing, crying, praying for a message saying you empathize...

But you don't.

Because in reality

You're tied up with someone and the thoughts of what can be

Wrapped up in her thickness and the lace of her panties.

In reality,

I'm forgotten. But sadly, it's you I can't forget.

So when I'm dismissed I take frequent trips to your inbox, because I don't want to be the source of your neglect.

But I'm neglected, and begging for your love and affection.

But I still look for a response... although it's rather inane, you see through my feelings like cellophane.

And even though it's been awhile, I can't accept the change—

Exposed

Change of heart, because in reality we're now apart.

You got me going in circles, round and round I go.

Praying it's not real, I don't want to accept what I know.

Now all I can do is think of what if and choke on words unspoken.

Knowing my perfect world is destroyed because in reality my heart is broken.

24- Why

Why?

Why am I in this predicament?

Laying here in the dark while my pillow's drenched.

Waiting for my phone to ring, but it's never who I want it to be.

Shallow words with hollow meaning

Wishing for things to be different from what they seem to be.

I allow you to hurt me, and I blame it on love.

I don't understand; this problem can't be solved.

I tie myself up, telling myself you love me.

But you don't.

I'm stuck holding on because I can't let go.

25- Just A Dream

I love you with my heart and soul

It's unexplainable, indescribable, but it's something that I know.

I can't breathe without you.

A bit dramatic, yeah I know, but I'm not complete when you go.

My dreams don't exist without you; I don't want anyone to love me but you.

It's your flaws that I love most.

Staring in your eyes give me hope;

If I said you could be replaced, when I'm spoiled by your love, I told a lie because it just isn't so.

You complete me.

I feel you in my dreams.

All the memories in my heart remind me what love really means.

I need you was what he said to me.

And it hurt so much, when I woke up, and it was all just a dream.

26- Slipping

I was caught slipping;

I tripped and fell directly in it.

I tried to brush it off, but it didn't come clean.

Now I'm delusional and I can't comprehend what it all means.

I'm shook.

My innocence was took—

Not my virginity but the vulnerability within me is now an open book, but I don't want it to be read.

I wish I could forget what was said.

I blame it on deception;

It always teaches the hardest of lessons.

Sometimes I wish I could forget it, erase every memory, but then I wonder if I'd live to regret it.

Is it really better to have loved than to never have loved at all?

Even if you fell and no one caught you just watched you trip and fall...

I must have bumped my head, because I'm trapped in this euphoric state.

I wasn't unscathed; I didn't fall into chaos this way. I've

changed.

I wasn't ready to evolve. I wanted things to stay the same

But now everything is altered. My feelings won't falter. I'm brainwashed by the ideal indelibly placed in my brain that I'll meet you at the altar.

But it's a lie

And all I can do is cry.

Because I was caught slipping and I tripped and fell in love.

27- My Red Lipstick

I hide behind my red lipstick.

Any pain I feel is diminished...

At least for the moment...

When I thought I was slipping, my red lipstick gave me the courage to hold it—

Or hold it in.

My mascara can't be smudged with tears; it would defeat the look that my red lipstick provided.

I'm able to express my feelings effortlessly. With lips this color, who could be silent?

I'm fine, is a lie that my red lipstick always tells.

Not caring for the moment is a task I do well.

While my lipstick is on

I feel invincible; I am capable to control my emotions.

Who really needs love when red symbolizes my devotion?

"Fuck you," sounds a lot sweeter when my red lipstick is on.

Don't try to guess, trust and believe my feelings won't be shown.

While my lips are red you'll never know what I'm dealing with,

Exposed

Because I'm not myself;

I hide behind my red lipstick.

28- I Apologize

I apologize for taking your love...

Leaving you confused and going from giving attention to none.

I apologize for all the lies I said while looking directly in your eyes and not caring about the compromise, because I was simply caring about what was between your thighs.

I apologize for painting an image that was distorted, hypothetical, and metaphoric.

It didn't actually include you, and now it's your heart that's contorted.

I apologize for the tears that I caused and me being the reason your soul is lost.

I apologize for saying I love you, I want you, and I need you,

Because the truth of the matter is I easily replaced you...

I apologize for believing you thought enough of me to give an apology.

Every empty promise you gave couldn't be repaired with "I'm sorry," but it's a start.

Any reason to dispel the pain in my heart,

To use me and make me fall for you, while you have bad intentions.

But you couldn't find one excuse to tell me to provide

positive deception?

So, I apologize

For loving you with every part of my heart,

And believing we would never be apart.

For believing I was the one

And thinking nothing could come between us

I apologize.

For hanging on your every word and closing my eyes so tight when we kissed.

I apologize for remembering you and wishing I was the one you missed.

But most of all, I apologize for praying for your apology.

29- Remember Me

Remember me smiling, the infectious laugh that I had

Forget all the bad.

Remember the good times instead.

Remember all the stupid things I did because they assisted in the makings of me.

Remember all the songs I sung loudly off key.

Remember those I loved, and how I loved hard.

And when I leave, just know I left everyone with a piece of my heart.

Learn from my mistakes because perfection was never in my description.

Remember my stubbornness, because sometimes I was quick to talk and not listen.

Remember my jokes; I hope they still make you laugh—

I hope you recite them whenever you feel sad.

Remember my look, because you can't tell me I didn't look good.

I would place my image indelibly in your mind if I could.

Remember my creativity, my personality, and all that jazz.

Remember that everything will be okay, and this too shall

pass.

I will always love you, so let go of the pain and sorrow.

Just let me live forever in your heart

All I ask is that you remember me tomorrow.

30- Just A Fuck

Just a fuck...

A long kiss and the simplicity of a touch

Never slow always rushed

Nothing more than infatuation nothing less than such

Conversations manufactured with the relatability of lies

Hurt hidden in tears of crying eyes

The truth of the matter cannot be denied

It's nothing more, nothing less—

Than sex

A lie wrapped in love to get you wet

A kiss to make you forget

Hate evolved into passion to make you vulnerable enough to penetrate

Never calming, always inundates

I'm overwhelmed with emotion, something he is lacking

Hoping our souls would intertwine and there would be more than us connecting while passing

In reality I just carry my idealistic expectations around like baggage

And pretend that love actually exists between us, and a

quick fuck isn't what just happened

After all, he could've chose anyone, but he chose me

It has to be love, not the fact that it was easy

In my head, it all makes sense

Fuck him till he falls, and when he does, he'll get dismissed

Trying to think like a man, but it is me at home crying like a bitch

I don't understand it

Maybe my comprehension is slightly off

If you don't want me, why waste time and make me fall?

Have me believing you're in love, when you clearly don't want to be involved

Just tell me the truth…

Be honest and just say this isn't love

I'm nothing more to you than a meaningless fuck.

31- Meant to be (incomplete)

Meant to be...could it all be that simple?

Blissful, carefree, loving—without playing on my mental

Exactly what is—not based on perception

Where experience is what teaches, not heart-breaking lessons.

Love is an action, not just said within a phrase.

It must be meant, said and shown within every passing day.

To feel needed, wanted, and as if you could never be replaced,

That there is no better, no panty too lace, that could ever take your place or make him turn the other way.

Real love is one that can't be measured.

It's more than a few dates, or a couple of fucks; it's a tie that can't be severed.

It's selfless, selfishness can't exist.

Love is happiness in seeing the smile on the one you love's face

And the butterflies you get after a kiss.

It's conversation when needed; it doesn't cower in defeat.

32- Come Back

In the corner of my mind, I can see it,

So vivid I can relive it.

I want to forget it,

But afraid to let go

Wishing this was a dream and you being gone isn't so.

I'm not content with this being the end;

Praying you'll come back and my heart will mend.

I see you when I close my eyes,

And I still smell you in my sheets.

Emotions run deep,

So I'd rather cry than speak.

I wish it could be simple

And you'd come back to me

Rather than dealing with you and these memories haunting me.

33- Willie Lynch is a Black Man

Willie Lynch is a black man;

272 years old still walking around this earth

Proving once and for all niggers ain't shit and using them for their worth—which ain't much of nothing.

Niggers are just disgusting, morally bankrupt, dependent and weak, used simply for production.

Niggers are being sold a dream, but ain't shit the way it seems.

Give a nigger an inch, he'll take a mile, but being a fool is the basis of slavery.

We are all still slaves, Willie Lynch is our master.

Martin Luther who? We ain't free; we're coons that created this disaster.

I have a dream that all this foolishness went away.

But I woke up and Willie wasn't lynching, he was bustin' niggers with AKs.

He had a couple of pickaninnies but for short he called them bitches.

Kept other niggers envious of his power and his riches;

That was his control—envy is greater than respect or admiration.

Make the strongest nigger a pussy and remove him from

his comfortable state of nature.

Break him down or even kill him in front of his woman so she'll see that he's bitch made.

She'll raise her daughters with strength and keep her sons afraid of being men and permanently in a weakened state.

Why do you think there are so many single mothers?

It's not a coincidence so many black women are stripping, wishing for a rich old white man to make it rain and provide them with better means of living.

Light skinned, dark skinned, we don't like or trust each other.

But that's the plan, since we ain't picking cotton; we ain't needed, so we're supposed to kill each other.

Killing "us" ain't a crime it's a badge of honor.

What's the point in making a difference today, if coons will fuck it up tomorrow?

34- Carrington and Cadence

I knew you before I met you.

We had a connection before I saw your face.

You were my ray of hope, any pain I felt, you made it magically go away.

You are the only thing I've done right.

You're truly the best thing in my life.

And if everything I did wrong or right gave me you, I'd do it again to have you by my side.

You are my princess.

It's my mission to make sure you never worry,

To help you realize your potential and to ensure that with any obstacle you face that you'll never get discouraged.

I can't always protect you from pain,

But I'll sure as hell try to mend your broken heart,

Assist you with living your dreams,

And encourage you to reach for the moon. Even if you fall short, you'll land among the stars.

You are so beautiful inside and out.

Confidence is key; always believe in yourself without a doubt.

Remember to learn from your lessons

Whether experience or in a book.

Intelligence is your life line, never rely solely on looks.

Proceed cautiously in life, give thought but never walk in fear.

Keep faith, never second guess your gut, and always remember...

I'll be near.

35- Goodbye

I wasn't ready to let go

Just give up on hope.

I wish I could just see your face just once more...

Or maybe just forget it.

Be a recipient of voluntary amnesia and can't remember it.

Erase all of the memories;

Scratch out all the laughs.

Forget all the times we made love,

No recollection of the reason I'm sad.

If I could move on, I believe I'd be fine.

But no one else is you, and it's your image that's trapped in my mind.

I can't forget you, believe me I tried.

When I'm awake at night it's evident I need you in my life,

But I can't have you...

So I pray for the courage to move on with my life,

Let go of your memory

And be content with goodbye.

A little something extra...

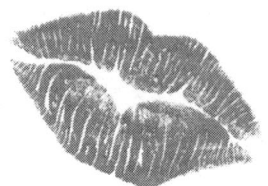

Because this book consists of my collected works, I wanted to include some things that I've written that aren't poetry. I understand that it is a faux pas to have something other than poetry in a "poetry book;" however, I will be the exception to the rule.

Men vs. Possums

There was a possum. On this one given day the possum was crossing the train tracks. A train was coming, horns blaring; the possum continued to cross the track. Barely making it, the possum made it across the track with only his tail cut off. Being a bit asinine the possum went back to get his tail...he was hit by the next train. He lost it all for a piece of tail.

Since, the beginnings of time men, like dogs and possums, have been chasing tail. Not thinking about the outcome just assuming that everyone will come out of the situation unscathed. But everyone knows that assuming makes an ass out of you, which in turn is the reason you have a problem. I couldn't help but wonder...is marriage until death do you part or until the next best thing comes along?

There are three sides to look at in this situation; the point of view of the man, his mistress, and his wife. The man's point of view is that he gets to have his cake and eat it too. The mistress simply believes that she is a girlfriend. All of the attention and gifts is just a perk of her new relationship. Majority of the time the mistress has no idea that her boyfriend is married, so there's no reason to confront her. Finally, you have the wife, who most likely knows it all. Men, don't ever underestimate your wife's intelligence; she most likely has you all figured out. She's hurt but being in love makes her suppress all of her emotions.

Looking at extramarital affairs the mistress gets better treatment than the wife. The man calls, texts, and emails this other woman to say he misses her. When they argue he begs for forgiveness. He dates her, takes her places he never takes his wife. He is basically having the ideal relationship with someone else.

On the other hand, the wife gets sporadic phone calls and an occasional "I love you." When they argue he cusses, fusses, and leaves. And dates are just names for the days on calendars. How is it that a female you've known all of five minutes gets better treatment than the woman you've supposedly devoted your life to?

Getting caught is all a part of cheating. All rats will be smelled, some truths made to lies, and skeletons will no longer be trapped in the closet. You've thought about this very moment, how people will be hurt, what will be said, etc. But honestly you didn't consider your wife. In your mind she's the stupid wife who sits at home waiting on you to get home from "work." The people, in your mind, that will feel pain is you and your mistress. Your wife's feelings aren't a priority, because if they were, you wouldn't do anything to hurt them. Look at it from her perspective; what if the tables were turned, would you be hurt?

I didn't write this to stereotype all men as cheaters. I honestly believe that there are some good men out there, but it's the bad apples that spoil the bunch. Growing old is inevitable, but growing up is optional. Life is full of choices, but it's obvious that these men are making wrong decisions. I wish that all of the good men would have a convention and grace the bad guys with some knowledge…but I know the chances of that actually happening. With that being said, I say this: to all men who cheat on your wives—or girlfriends for that matter, either do right by her or leave her alone. If you "love" her, cheating is not going to keep her with you. There will always be someone else that can do everything you do for her and won't cheat. If you devoted the same amount of time and effort you do to your mistress into your marriage, it would be blissful. However, if you continue to cheat on your wife, she may eventually leave you, and your mistress in turn will most likely do the same thing. You should never leave the one you love for the one you like, because the one you like will leave you for the one he or she loves. Don't be a relationship Robin Hood and give all of your riches to the poor.

You've heard the warning and made it across the tracks with only a cut tail; what do you do? Keep moving forward or turn around? Just ask yourself one question, is it all worth losing, over just a piece of tail?

Toxic Bachelors vs. Matrimony Males

Once upon a time, it seemed as though monogamy was as fictitious as the Easter bunny, and commitment was only existent in fairy tales. At one point, it seemed as though society was attempting to blackball the thought of exclusivity; but now, it seems as though committed relationships are becoming more prevalent. In a world that was once dominated by "toxic bachelors," women are now being introduced to a new breed, "matrimony males." Either society is turning over a new leaf and settling down is "in season" or "toxic bachelors" have become incognito and better liars.

"Toxic bachelors" are the worst men around. They are liars, cheaters, users, and abusers. "Toxic bachelors" are expert players and will always lie to women or whoever to get what they want. They will often use the same pick-up lines and rely heavily on their looks and fake charm to attract women. They are considered to be extremely shallow and only care about physical appearances. "Toxic bachelors" are typically good-looking well-dressed and are usually manipulative. Settling down is not in their repertoire and monogamy is a word that cannot be mentally assimilated.

"Matrimony males" are the relationship gurus. Although the "good guy" exterior may be misconstrued as game, the "matrimony male" has a genuinely good heart. His expectations are no longer, or may have never been, to get a woman to drop her panties on the first date, but to get to know her and possibly build a future with her. This group of males views marriage, kids, and a two story, blue shuttered house as a prominent goal in life.

    The dating scene, like fashion, is ever evolving but often repeats trends; the "matrimony males" are equivalent to the little black dress. They make you feel sexy, give you confidence, are flattering, and once you've found the perfect one for you, you hold on to it. As for "toxic bachelors" they're more along the lines of ultra-low-rise jeans. They aren't flattering for everyone and although you feel sexy at the moment, once you look in retrospect you find yourself exposed to the wrong crowd, feeling skanky and thinking, "this was a bad decision."

    Buyers beware—if you want to snag a "matrimony male," you have to look beyond the exterior and get past what's pleasing to the eye and seek what's pleasing to the heart. If not, you may end up with a "toxic bachelor." A "toxic bachelor" will tell you what you want to hear. However, a "matrimony male" will tell you the truth, whether or not it's what you want to hear, and hope you respect it. Shop accordingly.

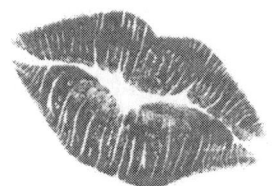

Society's effect on relationships:

Old School vs. New School

In many ways relationships have evolved over time. Some things that were once acceptable aren't anymore; and some things that were once valued are now depreciated. In so many ways things have changed, but was it because we as a people went through a transition, or because society made adjustments? When it comes to "old school" and "new school" relationships, why is there an apparent contrast?

Back in the day, times were very different. Not only was everything cheap, it was truly a man's world. Men brought home the bacon and women cooked it in the pan. For the most part, women leaned on men for practically everything; finances, intimacy, and because divorce was less common, women wanted to maintain a sense of normalcy. Although a lot of negative things may have occurred (i.e. cheating, beating, etc.) the couple always maintained their relationship; things were truly for better or worse.

Before the days of social media, there was a thing

called word-of-mouth, so it was easier to get away with having affairs if you could keep a secret. Men didn't flaunt their indiscretions out of "respect" for their spouse. Oftentimes if a man had a family outside of his marriage, it wasn't discussed, even if his spouse was aware of the situation. Counseling wasn't something that included a therapist; it was sleeping in separate beds until things showed improvement. Once upon of time, women truly held their men down; voluntarily or involuntarily. She didn't cheat regardless of his actions, cooked, cleaned, worked, raised children, and never complained. Although the "old school" method does demonstrate willful ignorance, it also shows that relationships should be non-disposable; which provides a type of stability that the younger generation is unaccustomed to.

In modern day, long lasting relationships are extremely rare. Society has made a way for women and men to co-exist in a world of opportunity. A woman can now bring home the bacon and cook it herself. Now that women can have hundreds of compatible men at her fingertips, thanks to dating sites, millions of sex toys for a low cost, and in vitro fertilization to create babies on her own, men have become non factors (to some woman); they are merely options. These days men are doing the same things they did years ago, they're just getting caught sooner because of the advancements in communication and because women have the "I can do bad all by myself mentality" relationships are ending abruptly.

If a marriage lasts beyond five years, it is considered to be shocking. In this day and age, relationships are disposable. Once upon a time, marriage was a goal, now it's seen as a curse. Women are more independent and correlate being submissive with being weak. Also, men don't have the same "respect" they used to, and often become careless. Vows are now just words that hold no validity; and oftentimes the bond between couples lack depth and substance barely reaching beyond a sexual nature. In a world of pre-nuptial agreements, divorce attorneys, and marriage counselors, it seems as though the smallest of problems are blown out of proportion causing things to be left unresolved; rather than things being worked out and used as a learning experience.

    It is quite evident that society has set the standards for how people respond in certain situations while in a relationship, but it is ultimately our decision for what the outcome may be. If we began to truly respect each other, as men and women, and stop taking each other for granted, it would be possible to experience a long lasting relationship. Regardless of what is perceived, love is unconditional and marriage shouldn't be disposable.

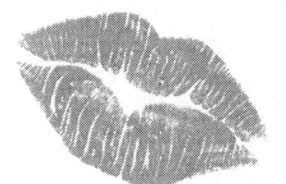

About the Author

Ireana Fields is a free spirit who has a passion for writing, drawing, acting, and familiarizing herself with African American history. After experiencing and accomplishing many things, she currently works in the medical field. Ireana has ghost written lyrics for select up and coming musical artists and samples of her writing have been featured on various websites. Although she spends a lot of her time reading, working, and writing, her primary focus is being a mother to her precocious daughters, Carrington and Cadence.

CPSIA information can be obtained at www.ICGtesting.com
Printed in the USA
LVOW12s2110110216

474769LV00001B/9/P